THE UNDERWATER WORLD OF SHARKS™

the SAND TIGER shark

Brad Burnham

The Rosen Publishing Group's
PowerKids Press™
New York

For my dad

Published in 2001 by The Rosen Publishing Group, Inc.
29 East 21st Street, New York, NY 10010

First Edition

Book Design: Maria Melendez

Photo Credits: Cover, title page, pp. 5, 6, 7, 11, 12, 16 © Peter Arnold, Inc.; p. 2, 3, 4, 22, 23, 24 © Animals, Animals; p. 8 © National Geographic; pp. 10, 11, 14, 15, 17, 18, 19, 20 © CORBIS-Bettmann; pp. 11, 12, 13, 19, 22 © Digital Stock; p. 21 © Bruce Watkins/Earth Scenes.

Burnham, Brad.
    The sand tiger shark/Brad Burnham.
        p. cm. — (The underwater world of sharks)
   Summary: Introduces the physical characteristics, behavior, habitat, and life cycle of the sand tiger shark.
    ISBN 0-8239-5707—1 (lb : alk. paper)
    1. Sand tiger shark–Juvenile literature. [1. Sand tiger shark. 2. Sharks.] I. Title. II. Series.

QL638.95.O3 B87 2000
597.3'4—dc21
                                99-059153

Contents

A Close LOOK

Sand tigers are large sharks that grow to be as long as 10 feet (3.05 m). The shape of their bodies is different from the shape of most sharks. Sand tigers are **hunched** in the middle. Their **snouts** are pointed. They have two large fins on their backs. These fins are called **dorsal** fins.

The skin color of a sand tiger shark is a grayish brown with dark spots. The shark's skin color changes as it gets older. Some of the spots fade away. The color of the sand tiger shark's skin is like the color of the sandy bottom of the ocean. The sand tiger's skin acts as **camouflage**. It helps keep the shark hidden as it swims along the ocean floor.

◀ *The sand tiger has skin that is the same color as the ocean floor. This helps the shark hide as it swims along.*

5

Gulping AIR

Most fish do not sink because they have an **air bladder** inside of them. An air bladder acts like a life preserver to help fish float. Sharks are fish, but they do not have air bladders. Most sharks sink if they stop swimming.

Sand tiger sharks have a different way to stop from sinking. They swallow air and keep it in their stomachs. The sharks swim to the surface of the ocean and gulp some air. Then they swim underwater and the air moves to their stomachs. Their stomachs act like an air bladder. Sand tiger sharks might be the only sharks that gulp air. No other kind of shark has ever been seen gulping air.

The sand tiger is the only shark that has been seen gulping air. ▶

Where Is HOME?

Sand tiger sharks live in the Atlantic and Pacific Oceans, and in the Mediterranean Sea. Large groups, or **schools**, of these sharks sometimes get together near the shores of North and South Carolina. Scientists think that the sharks gather in schools to hunt together or to find a **mate**.

In the summer, many sand tiger sharks swim near the shore between Cape Cod, Massachusetts, and the Delaware Bay. They stay in this area when the water is warm. When the water turns cold in the fall, the sharks move to warmer waters throughout the world. When an animal moves back and forth between two places each year it is called **migration**.

◀ *When the weather turns cold, sand tiger sharks move to warmer waters around the world.*

Sand tiger sharks are **predators**. Predators are animals that hunt other animals for food. Bluefish and bonito are two fast-swimming fish that sand tiger sharks hunt. Sand tiger sharks must be able to swim quickly to catch these fish. Sand tigers cannot swim fast for very long. Sometimes they do not catch the fish they are chasing.

Sand tigers do not eat every day. They might eat a lot one day and then nothing the next. They might eat as much as 100 pounds (37 kg) of food in one day. It might take a few days or even a week for a sand tiger shark to **digest** such a large meal.

Sand tigers like to eat bluefish and other small fish. ▶

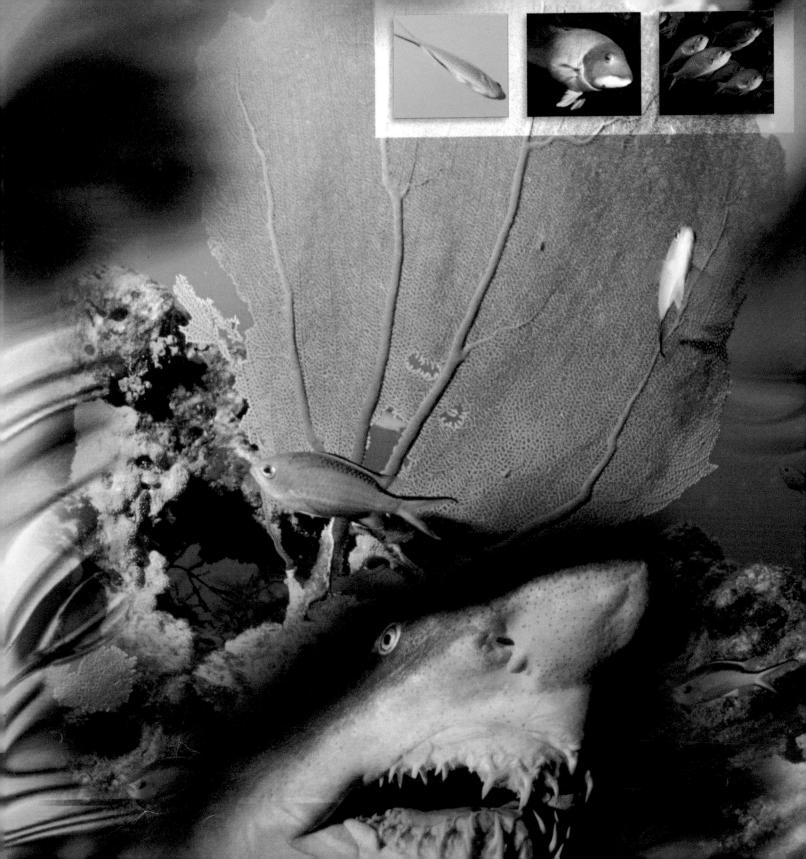

How Do SAND TIGERS Catch Their FOOD?

The animals that sharks hunt are called **prey**. Some sharks hide and wait for small fish to swim by them. Sharks that are fast can chase their prey. Sand tigers can chase a fast fish for a short distance. They can also **ambush** their prey by attacking it from behind.

People have seen sand tiger sharks swimming near schools of fish. The sharks swim around the fish. Then they rush into the middle of the school. They snap at the fish with their jaws. Sometimes the sharks only **injure** one of the fish. A fish that is injured is easier to catch.

◀ *Sand tiger sharks will rush into a school of fish, snapping at them with their powerful jaws.*

Snaggle **TOOTH**

Sand tiger sharks have long, curved teeth. The shark's teeth have this shape to help them hold onto their food. The sand tiger's teeth are like the **prongs** of a fork. A fish caught in a sand tiger shark's mouth might struggle but will probably not get away. The teeth of a sand tiger shark are not good for taking bites out of large prey. Sand tigers cannot tear or shred flesh, so they have to swallow their prey whole.

Sand tigers use their sharp teeth to hold onto their prey. ▶

Having BABIES

Some kinds of sharks lay eggs. Other kinds keep their eggs inside their bodies until their babies are ready to be born. The eggs **develop** inside of the mother. Sand tiger sharks keep their eggs inside of their bodies for 9 to 12 months.

There are many eggs inside of the mother but only two **hatch**, or come out from their eggs. They hatch out of the eggs but stay in the mother. These two babies eat yolk from their eggs to help them grow. The yolk is stored in a sack called a yolk sac. The babies also eat the eggs that do not hatch. The babies, called **pups**, do not hurt their mother when they eat the eggs.

The pups in these pictures are shown attached to their yolk sacs. The yolk sacs provide food for the pups as they develop.

17

In different parts of the world sand tiger sharks are known by different names. In some parts of North America they are called sand sharks. People in South Africa call sand tiger sharks ragged-tooth sharks because of the shape of their teeth.

In Australia sand tiger sharks are called gray nurse sharks. This is because sand tiger sharks have a shape and color a lot like a shark called a nurse shark. Scientists use the Latin name **Odontaspis taurus** for sand tiger sharks. In English *Odontaspis* means "snake tooth."

Sand tigers look a lot like the nurse shark pictured here. In Australia, sand tigers are called gray nurse sharks. ▶

Sand Tigers and PEOPLE

Sand tiger sharks are considered dangerous in Australia. Some people in Australia have been attacked by sand tigers. Sand tiger sharks are not considered dangerous in North America. Scientists do not know why the sharks attack in one part of the world, but not in the other.

People can be dangerous to sharks, too. We fish for them with fishing poles or with nets. Many sharks are caught by accident when people try to catch other kinds of fish. The United States has passed fishing laws that are meant to protect sand tigers and other kinds of sharks. If we keep protecting sand tiger sharks, hopefully they will not become **endangered**.

◀ *We must protect sharks, not hunt them. If we obey fishing laws we can stop sand tigers and other sharks from becoming endangered.*

At the AQUARIUM

Many aquariums have sand tiger sharks swimming in their tanks. Some sharks cannot **adapt** to living in an aquarium tank. Sand tiger sharks can adapt. They can change the amount of energy they use and slow down their activity. This makes them able to live in tanks. Visitors at aquariums like to look into the mouths of sand tigers and see all of their sharp teeth. Scientists also watch sand tiger sharks at aquariums. By watching them in their tanks, they learned how sand tigers gulp air. They also learned how much food a sand tiger needs to keep up its energy level. As we find out more about sand tigers and other sharks, we can learn better ways to live with them.

Glossary

adapt (uh-DAPT) To change to fit new conditions.

air bladder (ayr-BLA-der) An air-filled pouch in the body of fish with bones.

ambush (AM-bush) To attack by surprise.

camouflage (KA-muh-flaj) The color or pattern of an animal's feathers, fur, or skin that helps it blend into its surroundings.

develop (dih-VEH-lup) To grow or expand.

digest (dy-JEST) When your body breaks down the food you eat to use for energy.

dorsal (DOR-sel) Positioned on the back.

endangered (en-DAYN-jerd) When something is in danger of no longer existing.

hatch (HATCH) To come out from an egg.

hunched (HUNCHT) To be bent in a crooked position.

injure (IN-jur) To harm or damage.

mate (MAYT) One of a pair of animals that join together to make babies.

migration (my-GRAY-shun) When large groups of animals or people move from one place to another.

Odontaspis taurus (oh-don-TAS-pis TOR-us) The scientific name for sand tiger sharks.

predators (PREH-duh-terz) Animals that kill other animals for food.

prey (PRAY) An animal that is eaten by another animal for food.

prongs (PRONGZ) One of the pointed ends of a fork.

pups (PUPS) A type of baby animal.

schools (SKOOLZ) Groups of fish.

snouts (SNOWTS) Parts of animal heads that include the nose, mouth, and jaw.

Index

Web Sites:

To find out more about sand tiger sharks, check out these Web sites:
http://www.occs.com/sandtigersharks
http://www.postmodern.com/~fi/sharkpics/ellis/sandtigr.htm